Mother Teresa

A LIFE OF CARING

by Robin Nelson

Lerner Publications Company • Minneapolis

Photo Acknowledgments

The photographs in this book are reproduced with the permission of: © Louise Gubb/The Image Works, front cover; © Raghu Rai/Magnum Photos, pp. 4, 25; Don Lush Gjergji, pp. 6, 8, 9, 10; © Earl & Nazima Kowall/CORBIS, p. 12; AP/Wide World Photos, pp. 13, 14, 26; © Kapoor Baldev/Sygma/CORBIS, pp. 16, 17, 21; © SUCHETA DAS/Reuters/Corbis, p. 18; © DESHAKALYAN CHOWDHURY/AFP/Getty Images, p. 20; © Bettmann/CORBIS, p. 22; © JP Laffont/Sygma/CORBIS, pp. 23, 24; ©STR/AFP/Getty Images, p. 27.

Lerner Publications Company
A division of Lerner Publishing Group
241 First Avenue North
Minneapolis, MN 55401 U.S.A.

Website address: www.lernerbooks.com

Words in **bold type** are explained in a glossary on page 31.

Library of Congress Cataloging-in-Publication Data

Nelson, Robin, 1971–
    Mother Teresa : a life of caring / by Robin Nelson.
        p.   cm. —   (Pull ahead books)
    Includes index.
    ISBN-13: 978-0-8225-6384-6 (lib. bdg. : alk. paper)
    ISBN-10: 0-8225-6384-3 (lib. bdg. : alk. paper)
        1. Teresa, Mother, 1910–1997–Juvenile literature.   2. Missionaries of Charity–
Biography–Juvenile literature.   3. Nuns–India–Calcutta–Biography–Juvenile literature.   I.
Title.   II. Series.
    BX4406.5.Z8N45 2007
    271'.97–dc22   2006002238

Manufactured in the United States of America
1 2 3 4 5 6 – JR – 12 11 10 09 08 07

Table of Contents

A Caring Mother

Mother Teresa spent her life **caring** for people. She helped children learn. She gave food to people who were hungry and poor. She gave medicine to people who were sick. She took care of people who were dying.

Young Agnes and her mother

A Caring Child

Mother Teresa's name was Agnes when she was growing up in Europe. Agnes was always a caring person. She helped care for sick neighbors. She helped a woman take care of her children. She helped her mother feed hungry strangers.

Agnes (second from left) with her classmates

Agnes spent a lot of time at her
church. She went to the church
school. She sang in the church **choir**.

When Agnes was 12 years old, she decided that she would become a **nun**. A nun is a woman who gives up everything to serve the church.

Agnes (back row on the right) with other nuns

Young Sister Teresa

Sister Teresa

Agnes joined a **convent** when she was 18 years old. She lived in the convent with nuns. She learned to be a nun. Then she moved to India. Agnes became a nun and changed her name to Sister Teresa.

Indian children look for food.

Sister Teresa had everything she
needed in her convent in India. But
many Indian people were very **poor**.

The poor lived in **huts** with mud floors. They did not have enough food. Their clothes were rags. Sister Teresa wanted to help them.

Children play outside a hut.

Poor people sit on the street in Calcutta.

Caring for the Poor

Sister Teresa left the convent. She went to live with the poor people she wanted to help. Sister Teresa lived in the **slums** of Calcutta, India. Slums are very poor areas of a city.

Sister Teresa with children in Calcutta

In the slums, Sister Teresa taught the children.

She gave medicine to the sick.

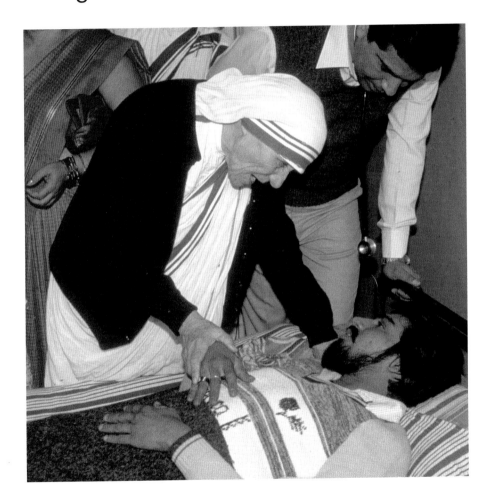

Mother Teresa's nuns were called the Missionaries of Charity.

Mother to All

Soon other nuns came to help Sister Teresa. Sister Teresa started her own group of nuns. Sister Teresa became Mother Teresa.

These nuns worked with Mother Teresa to help the poor.

Mother Teresa and her nuns moved into a house together. They slept, ate, and prayed at their house.

But they spent most of their days in the streets helping people.

Mother Teresa saw many people dying in Calcutta's streets. Hospitals would not help these people because they could not pay.

Mother Teresa opened a house to care for poor people who were dying. She believed that everyone should be cared for and loved.

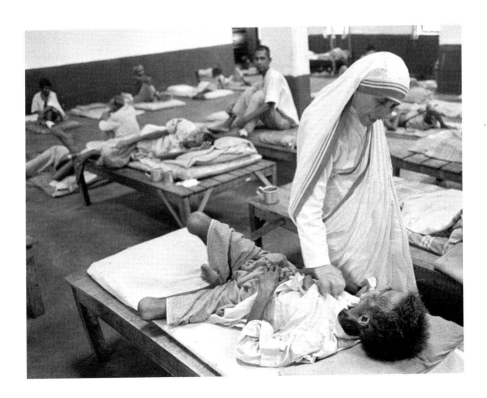

Mother Teresa also opened a home for **orphans**. These are babies and children who do not have parents.

Some of these children were very sick. Mother Teresa cared for them and treated them as if they were her own family.

Mother Teresa wins the Nobel Peace Prize.

In 1979, Mother Teresa received an important award for her work with the poor.

Mother Teresa said that no one should feel unwanted. She cared about all people. She showed kindness and love to everyone.

MOTHER TERESA TIMELINE

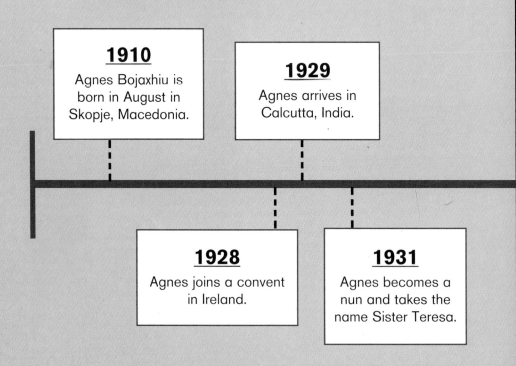

1910
Agnes Bojaxhiu is born in August in Skopje, Macedonia.

1929
Agnes arrives in Calcutta, India.

1928
Agnes joins a convent in Ireland.

1931
Agnes becomes a nun and takes the name Sister Teresa.

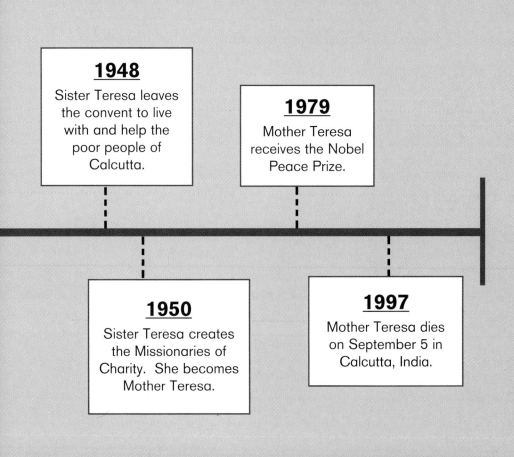

1948
Sister Teresa leaves the convent to live with and help the poor people of Calcutta.

1979
Mother Teresa receives the Nobel Peace Prize.

1950
Sister Teresa creates the Missionaries of Charity. She becomes Mother Teresa.

1997
Mother Teresa dies on September 5 in Calcutta, India.

More about Mother Teresa

● Mother Teresa started her first school in the slums by gathering children under a tree. She taught them the alphabet by writing the letters in the dirt with a stick.

● When Mother Teresa won the Nobel Peace Prize, she used all the money she received to help the poor.

● Mother Teresa helped open houses all over the world to help the poor and sick.

Websites

Mother Teresa–Biography
http://nobelprize.org/peace/laureates/1979/teresa-bio.html

Mother Teresa of Calcutta: Peacemaker, Pioneer, Legend
http://www.ewtn.com/motherteresa/

A Tribute to the "Saint of the Gutters"
http://www.cnn.com/WORLD/9709/mother.teresa/

Glossary

caring: showing concern for others

choir: a group of singers

church: a Christian house of worship

convent: a house for a group of nuns

huts: simple, small houses. Some huts are made of mud or grass.

nun: a woman who gives up everything to serve the Catholic church

orphans: children who do not have parents

poor: not having much money

slums: a very poor, crowded area of a city

Index